evangelization is not a dirty word.

"Clear, concise, practical, and encouraging – just the resource we need for the New Evangelization."

Brandon Vogt
Author of *Church and New Media*

"If you have ever wanted to know what the Church teaches about evangelization but didn't know where to start, start here."

Tony Vasinda
Co-Founder of *ProjectYM*

THE **E** WORD

MICHAEL MARCHAND

The E Word – Third Edition
© Copyright 2016 Michael Marchand. All rights reserved.

ISBN 978-1-300-04160-3
PUBLISHED BY PROJECTYM.COM

CONTENTS

The What?	1
The Why?	7
The Who?	15
The Where?	23
The How?	35
The Result?	45

Share your thoughts as you read through the book on Facebook, Twitter and Instagram
#TheEWord

though
THE
WHAT?

A DIRTY WORD.

I'm a cradle Catholic and a product of Catholic school (elementary, middle school, high school, even college). Every day of my academic life, time was spent learning about the teachings of the Church.

We learned about saints, Sacraments, schisms, Scripture, shrines, sin, stigmata, synods, sacrilege and scapulars. We learned when to kneel, when to sit, when to genuflect, when to bow, when to strike our chest, when to cross our lips, and when to stand. We learned what to believe, how to behave, and where we belong.

As I think back on those hours of learning what it means to be Catholic, I cannot remember ever talking about evangelization. I can't even remember a single teacher ever just saying the word "evangelization"[1].

It was as if "evangelization" was a dirty word.

IT SOUNDS PROTESTANT.

For starters, the word alone sounds too Protestant for a lot of Catholics (maybe it's just too close to the word "evangelical"). Even beyond the word, far too many Catholics would say that the idea of telling people about their faith is just too preachy, too pushy, too Protestant. And for some reason, we Catholics are so afraid of that label.

---

[1] **Full disclosure:** We talked about the Evangelists (Matthew, Mark, Luke, John), but that was always a title attributed to them alone. The idea that we might be called to be evangelists was definitely never discussed.

EVANGELIZATION DEFINED.

Since you probably never learned this in school either, I figured the best way to begin a book on evangelization was to define it. Rather than just give you my definition, I thought we'd see what people smarter than me say it is:

> **"Evangelization means to set out with Christ in order to pass on the gift we have received, to transform poverty of every kind."**
>
> *Cardinal Ratzinger* [2]

> **"For the Church, evangelizing means bringing the Good News into all the strata of humanity, and through its influence transforming humanity from within and making it new."**
>
> *Pope Paul VI* [3]

It seems for both Cardinal Ratzinger (aka Pope Benedict XVI) and Pope Paul VI, there are two essential components of evangelization:

1. Bringing the gift of the Word into the world.
2. Transforming the world it's brought into.

Simply put, evangelization is sharing the Word of God to transform the world.

---

[2] Joseph Cardinal Ratzinger, Gospel, Catechesis, Catechism, p. 44

[3] Pope Paul VI, Evangelii Nuntiandi, 18

A KICK IN THE BUTT.

St. John Paul II believed in the importance of and the need for evangelization so much that he made it one of the main focuses of his pontificate.[4]

Why? Because when John Paul II took a look around, he saw that the world needed the transforming Word of God, and the Church should be stepping up her efforts to bring that Word into the world. Quite frankly, he was saying that our evangelization needed a swift kick in the butt.

In an encyclical entitled *Redemptoris Missio* (or "Mission of the Redeemer"), John Paul II "invite[d] the Church to renew her missionary commitment"[5]. Wanting to establish a sense of urgency and importance, he went even further and called the Church to a new evangelization:

> **"I sense that the moment has come to convert all of the Church's energies to a new evangelization."**
>
> *St. John Paul II* [6]

John Paul II was throwing all his weight and "all of the Church's energies" behind this mission. He was declaring just how important this new evangelization was and just how desperate the world was for the Gospel.

---

[4] United States Conference of Catholic Bishops, Committee on Evangelization and Catechesis, "Disciples Called to Witness: The New Evangelization"

[5] St. John Paul II, Redemptoris Missio, 2

[6] St. John Paul II, Redemptoris Missio, 3

WHAT DO YOU MEAN "NEW"?

John Paul II explains that this new evangelization is "new in its ardour, new in its methods, and new in its means of expression"[7]. It's a calling for the Church to evangelize with renewed passion; modern, relevant methods; and a desire to transform the world.

CHECKING OUR VITALS.

It's easy to understand when an apple tree is healthy: if it's producing apples, it's healthy. The more apples it produces, the healthier the apple tree.

What about the Church? How do we know when she is healthy? What are the indicators? St. John Paul II explains that when the Church is healthy, she produces missionaries (people embracing their call to evangelize).

> **"Missionary drive has always been a sign of vitality, just as its lessening is a sign of crisis of faith."**
>
> *St. John Paul II* [8]

Take a look at the Church, would you say she is producing missionaries? Is she instilling a missionary in the faithful? What does that say about her health?

What about you? If our willingness to evangelize is "an accurate indicator of our faith in Christ and his love for us"[9], how would you rate your faith?

---

[7] St. John Paul II, "Address to the Bishops of Latin America" (Haiti, 1983)

[8] St. John Paul II, *Repemtoris Missio*, 2

[9] St. John Paul II, Repemtoris Missio, 2

THE WHY?

BECAUSE JESUS SAYS SO.

The book of Acts opens on the Apostles waiting. Why? Because Jesus told them to and a good Apostle knows how to follow directions.

After Jesus rises from the dead, He spends 40 days hanging out with His disciples, His friends. He spends 40 days "speaking about the kingdom of God" and the "promise of the Father"[10]. So the Apostles are simply waiting on the Father to deliver on this promise.

What? Before Jesus ascends into heaven, He promises his disciples that He will send them "power from on high"[11], or as we call Him "the Holy Spirit".

They did more than just wait around: they prayed. Gathered together in an upper room, the earliest leaders of the Church spent their time, day and night, in prayer: preparing for what God was going to do through them. Then it happens. The Father delivers.

> **"And suddenly there came from the sky a noise like a strong driving wind, and it filled the entire house in which they were. Then there appeared to them tongues as of fire, which parted and came to rest on each one of them. And they were all filled with the holy Spirit"**
> *Acts 2:2-4*

The story doesn't end there. The Spirit filled each one of them for a very specific purpose. There was more to

---

[10] Acts 1:3; Acts 1:4, Luke 24:49

[11] Luke 24:49

this promise than just an extraordinary gift. This gift came with a command[12].

> **"But you will receive power when the Holy Spirit comes upon you, and you will be my witnesses in Jerusalem, throughout Judea and Samaria, and to the ends of the earth."**
>
> *Acts 1:8*

Power? Yeah, I'll take that. Holy Spirit? Sure! Witnesses to the ends of the earth? Sounds like a job for someone else, right?

Wrong. The promise and command Jesus gave to the Apostles, He gives to us. We have each been given the power of the Holy Spirit (even if a "strong driving wind" has never filled your house), and we have each been called, commanded to be Christ's witness "to the ends of the earth".

Why do we evangelize? Because Jesus says so. Not just in Acts, but throughout the Gospels as well[13].

BECAUSE THE CHURCH SAYS SO.

Did you ever ask your dad for permission to do something only to get shot down? Most of us respond to such defeat by changing our target: we ask Mom. It only took a "Yes" from one or the other for us to feel justified in doing whatever it was we were hoping to do.

---

[12] **Helpful hint:** Jesus doesn't give suggestions. If He tells you to do something, it's always a command.

[13] Mt 28:18-20, Mk 16:15-18, Lk 24:46-49, Jn 20:21-23

But when both parents came back with the same response and the same instructions even when they were asked separately, we knew there was no chance of appeal.

Jesus very clearly tells us we're supposed to evangelize, and his bride, the Church, tells us the exact same thing. She even uses stronger words than Him:

> **"The task of evangelizing all people constitutes the essential mission of the Church. It is a task and mission which the vast and profound changes of present-day society make all the more urgent. Evangelizing is in fact the grace and vocation proper to the Church, her deepest identity. She exists in order to evangelize"**
>
> *Pope Paul VI* [14]

Don't miss that last sentence: the Church exists to evangelize. It's not just one the things that the Church should do, it is THE thing she MUST do. If she exists to evangelize, if that is her deepest identity, then if she's not evangelizing, there is no reason for the Church to exist.

If we are the Church, the body of Christ, then the mission of the Church is our mission. If the Church exists in order to evangelize, then that should be the very reason for our existence as well. No excuses.

---

[14] Pope Paul VI, Evangelii Nuntiandi, 14

> **"No believer in Christ, no institution of the Church can avoid this supreme duty: to proclaim Christ to all peoples."**
>
> *St. John Paul II* [15]

> **"To be a Christian and to be a missionary is the same thing."**
>
> *Pope Francis* [16]

Far too often we look at evangelization as optional. We tell ourselves: "Those people who are good at evangelization should do that, that's not really my gift, so God can't expect me to do something that I'm not good at. He can't really want me to do something I don't like doing. Right?"

Wrong:

> **"All the Christian faithful...are bound by the general obligation...to work so that the divine message of salvation is made known and accepted by all persons everywhere in the world."**
>
> *Code of Canon Law, 225*

Did you catch that? Canon Law says "<u>*All the Christian faithful*</u>", not "those who are good at sharing their faith" or "people who love to evangelize". No, the same obligation to preach the Gospel that was imposed on Paul[17], has been imposed on all of us.

---

[15] St. John Paul II, Repemtoris Missio, 3

[16] Pope Francis, Angelus, January 24, 2014

[17] 1 Corinthians 9:16

The Church doesn't mince words. If we believe in Christ, evangelization is our duty, our obligation. It should be the reason for our existence.

BECAUSE IT'S NECESSARY.

There's more to it than obligation. It's more than simply doing what we're told. Evangelization is doing what needs to be done.

> **"The presentation of the Gospel message is not an optional contribution for the Church...this message is indeed necessary. It is unique. It cannot be replaced...It is a question of people's salvation."**
>
> *Pope Paul VI* [18]

There are millions and millions of people that have never heard about the love and sacrifice of Christ, and that number "is constantly on the increase"[19]. These people need to hear the Gospel.

We should respond to this need not out of a sense of duty or obligation but simply because there is a need that we can fill. If the world needs Christ, and we know Christ, sharing Him with the world should be our natural reaction.

The question isn't: Is there a need? We know there's a need. The question we should be asking is: What are we going to do to fulfill that need?

---

[18] Pope Paul VI, Evangelii Nuntiandi, 5

[19] St. John Paul II, Repemtoris Missio, 3

BECAUSE WE CAN'T HELP IT.

Have you ever overheard a group of people talking about your favorite band and you just had to chime in? Have you ever seen a movie that was so incredible that you told people about it any chance you could? Have you ever recommended a restaurant because the food was just that good? Have you ever worn a jersey to show the world how much you love a particular team (especially when you knew you'd be around fans of the team they beat last night)?

There are things in life we can't help but talk about. Things we can't help but share with others. Our relationship with Christ should be one of those things. When we truly encounter Him, when we let Him take over our whole life, Jesus is incredibly contagious.

> **"The person who has been evangelized goes on to evangelize others...it is unthinkable that a person should accept the Word and give himself to the kingdom without becoming a person who bears witness to it and proclaims it in his turn."**
>
> *Pope Paul VI* [20]

Peter and John are perfect examples of this.

In the book of Acts, we find Peter and John touring Jerusalem proclaiming the name of Jesus, telling people of His marvelous deeds, healing in His name, and sharing with everyone they meet about their relationship with Christ. The Sanhedrin (read as "the

---

[20] Pope Paul VI, Evangelii Nuntiandi, 24

relationship with Christ. The Sanhedrin (read as "the bad guys") pull them in and tell them to stop: stop preaching, stop healing, stop speaking the name of Jesus. Or else.

Peter and John's response is evidence of their relationship with Christ:

> **"It is impossible for us not to speak about what we have seen and heard."**
> *Acts 4:20*

They had an encounter with Jesus, they walked with Him, learned from Him, witnessed His power, and built a relationship with Him. Keeping that experience to themselves was no longer an option. They had to talk about it! They had to share it with everyone they met! The bad guys couldn't stop them.

What about you? Who's stopping you? Who or what are the bad guys in your life? Fear? Pride? Doubt?

If you have a real relationship with Christ, you should be busting at the seams to tell the world about it. That seems like a good way to measure what most people claim is immeasurable: faith. If your faith is strong enough, nothing should be able to stop you from sharing it.

THE WHO?

YOU. ME. EVERYONE.

God created us "in His image"[21]. He didn't intend for us to hide this image. He didn't intend for us to conceal our Creator. God created us to be reflections of His glory. He created us so that when other people saw us, they would see Him!

Most of us wouldn't argue with that statement. Sure, God created us to reflect His glory. We'll gladly stand there and let God radiate glory: we're not afraid to take on such a passive role. But unfortunately (or fortunately), God created us to do more than just be a mirror. He created each one of us to go out and "make disciples of all nations"[22].

Go. Make. Those are not passive words. Those are action words, words that get us up off our couch and out sharing our faith[23].

> **"Every Christian is challenged, here and now, to be actively engaged in evangelization; indeed, anyone who has truly experienced God's saving love does not need much time or lengthy training to go out and proclaim that love."**
>
> *Pope Francis* [24]

---

[21] Genesis 1:27

[22] Matthew 28:19

[23] **Random pop culture reference:** "That's the action word that gets the subject up and out." ("The Tale of Mr Morton", School House Rock)

[24] Pope Francis, Evangelii Gaudium, 120

There's no way around it: if we call ourselves followers of Christ, going out and making disciples is part of the job description.

UNQUALIFIED? IRRELEVANT.

As soon as people hear that they're supposed to "go make disciples", the excuses start flying: That's just not me. That's not one of my gifts. There are other people way better at that kind of thing. I'm an introvert. I don't know enough about my faith. I'm unqualified.

The fact is, each one of those excuses is irrelevant.

That's just not me.
Actually, yes it is. That it is EXACTLY who God created you to be. You are an evangelist by God's design. God created you for two primary purposes: To be in relationship with Him and to bring other people into relationship with Him. And besides, you didn't choose this role, God chose you for this job:

> **"It was not you who chose me, but I who chose you and appointed you to go and bear fruit that will remain"**
>
> *John 15:16*

That's not one of my gifts.
Guess what? You don't have to do this alone. None of us do. If we keep reading in Matthew, right after Jesus tells us to go out and make disciples, He makes us a promise: "I am with you always"[25]. That's right, whenever we go out to evangelize, He is with us. When

---

[25] Matthew 18:20

we open our mouth to speak the Gospel, He is with us (sometimes He even places the words in our mouth)[26]. When we reach out to build up disciples, He is with us.

Even if evangelization isn't your gift, even if you'd go so far as to say it's one of your weaknesses:

"[His] strength is made perfect in your weakness"

2 Corinthians 12:9

There are other people better at that kind of thing.
You're right. And you know what? You'll probably mess up sometimes. You'll probably straight-up fail sometimes.

So it's a good thing our God doesn't demand perfection. It's a good thing He doesn't demand success.

"God doesn't ask that we succeed in everything, but that we are faithful."

St. Theresa of Calcutta

So it doesn't matter if other people are better at evangelizing than you, because God has called YOU to do it. The question is: are you being faithful to that calling?

"Remain faithful until death, and I will give you the crown of life."

Revelation 2:10

---

[26] Jeremiah 1:9

I'm an introvert.
So was Moses, and he led an entire nation out of slavery.

So was Amos, and he spoke out against the sins of an entire empire.

If God can do great things through them, reach huge numbers of people through them, then your introversion does not disqualify you from evangelizing.

In fact, it might even open doors for you that would never be open to extrovert. Think about it introverts, who would you rather talk to: a fellow introvert or an over-the-top extrovert?

Embrace your gift and use it to build the kingdom.

> **"As each one has received a gift, use it to serve one another."**
>
> *1 Peter 4:10*

I don't know enough about my faith.
That's true, you don't. I don't. Your priest doesn't. And you know what? We never will.

Faith formation is supposed to be lifelong: meaning every day of your life you should be learning more about your faith and deepening your relationship with Christ. Every day.

More importantly: You don't need to be a theology expert to follow Christ. You don't need to be a theologian to share your love for Him.

> **"We evangelize not with grand words, or complicated concepts, but with 'the joy of the Gospel' which 'fills the hearts and lives of all who encounter Jesus' "**
>
> *Pope Francis* [27]

Peter wasn't an expert, far from it. Peter was a simple, uneducated fisherman, and he was one of the boldest, most effective evangelists in the history of Christianity – leading thousands of people to Jesus and the Church.

I'm unqualified.
The great thing about that excuse is that it's actually the reason your testimony is so powerful. We don't often listen to people we see as "Jesus experts".

We don't relate to them, we don't connect with them. They're over qualified.

It is so much more powerful when we hear imperfect, unqualified people share about their love for God. Even more so when we manage to catch a glimpse of God active in their life: because that's when we realize that if God can work through the unqualified, He can work through us too.

> **"You may not be an evangelism expert and you may not have gone to seminary, but you may well be the most qualified person to share Christ with the people in your world."**
>
> *Steve Douglass* [28]

---

[27] Pope Francis, Mass for the Evangelization of Peoples on July 7, 2015

[28] Steve Douglass, "A Unique Advantage"

NO PERFECT PEOPLE ALLOWED.

God's glory is most evident in our salvation. Why? Because we don't deserve it, we didn't earn it. So if God has the power to save us, imperfect as we are, how much greater does that make God? A god who saves and reconciles perfect people is not all that impressive. I mean, let's be honest, I could make a perfect person look perfect.

But the story of God transforming our imperfections: that's power. God using sinners to give witness to His glory: that's worth hearing.

No one wants to hear about how God has blessed perfect people. People want to know how God is active in the lives of real people. People want to see how Christ has transformed lives.

Perfect people can't be transformed, broken people can. So share your brokenness. Share your imperfections.

And give God all the glory for your successes.

THE WHERE?

CAN YOU DRAW ME A MAP?

If we accept the fact that we're supposed to evangelize, we're left with an important question: WHERE?

I mean, Jesus doesn't expect us all to stand on the sidewalk and just start preaching, does He? And that verse from the beginning of Acts isn't really any help on this either. He seems to be telling us to hop on a plane and fly to Israel:

> **"You will be my witnesses in Jerusalem, throughout Judea and Samaria, and to the ends of the earth."**
>
> *Acts 1:8*

Surely He's not saying everyone needs to go preach the Gospel in Jerusalem, right? So then how do we take those words and apply it to our individual situations?

When He said those words, Jesus was speaking to each one of us, but also to the apostles He was standing in front of. So a good way to start understanding what these words mean for us is to understand what they meant for the Apostles.

Jesus was calling His disciples to preach the Gospel in their home town (Jerusalem), in the surrounding areas (Judea and Samaria), and to the "ends of the earth".

To take it a step further, Jesus was calling them to preach first where they are the most comfortable[29],

---

[29] Maybe **comfortable** is the wrong word. If you're like me, you'd say it is extremely uncomfortable to share your faith with those you're closest too. Close friends and family members can sometimes be very intimidating when it comes to faith-sharing. It shouldn't be, but it is. Maybe a better word choice is ***familiar***.

with the people they know the best, the people they have the closest relationships with.

Then, once they've done that, to step out a little bit and share the Gospel in places they're not as familiar with. He wasn't sending them to brand new, unknown places (yet).

He was asking them to take a small step out of their comfort zone, away from the people they know and love, and into something a little less familiar, a little less comfortable.

But once both those boxes have been checked, Jesus gives them an audacious goal: preach the gospel "to the ends of the earth"!

Throw comfort zones out the window and go where you've never gone before. Share your faith with people you've never met!

That's our map: start with your inner circle (people and places you're the most comfortable with), and slowly expand that circle until you've reached "the ends of the earth".

Easier said then done, right?

Maybe if we get a little more specific?

YOUR SPHERE OF INFLUENCE.

We all have one. Some folks have a huge list of people who listen to them, respect them. For others that list is much shorter. But regardless of the length of the list, our responsibility is the same: to point those people to Jesus.

John the Baptist took this responsibility to heart.

Everything he did was about pointing people to Jesus. His entire mission was to step back from the spotlight so Christ would shine. So Jesus would get the glory:

"He must increase; I must decrease."

John 3:30

Those were actually the last words of John the Baptist recorded in the Gospel of John. How fitting that his last words declare that he must decrease so that God can get ALL the glory.

Even before that statement, John the Baptist took the initiative to point people to Jesus any chance he got – sometimes literally.

One day on the banks of the Jordan River, John is preaching and Jesus walks by. John stops and points out to his followers:

"Behold, the Lamb of God, who takes away the sin of the world."

John 1:29

The very next day, John is hanging out with two of his disciples and "as he watched Jesus walk by", John again points to Jesus saying:

"Behold, the Lamb of God."

John 1:36

How are you using your influence?

When people look to you, do you point them back to yourself, or do you point them to Jesus?

When others see that things are going well in your life, are you taking the glory or giving it all to God?

YOUR FAMILY.

When the John the Baptist points out Jesus, the Lamb of God, to his two disciples that day, the two of them pick up and follow after Jesus.

They don't say anything, they just get up and go. After they've been following Jesus around like a puppy for a few minutes, Jesus turns to them and asks (quite bluntly):

> **"What are you looking for?"**
>
> *John 1:38*

The two disciples are caught off guard.

Not sure how to respond, they come up with an incredibly random question, "Where are you staying?"

Jesus invites them to come with Him and see for themselves. So they do, and they hang out with Jesus the rest of the afternoon.

But after that encounter, after that time with Jesus, one of those two disciples, Andrew, decided He needed to do more than just sit in Jesus' presence, he needed to go and tell someone about Him:

> **"The first thing Andrew did was to find his brother Simon and tell him, 'We have found the Messiah.' "**
>
> *John 1:41 [NIV]*

Andrew leaves Jesus' presence and *the very first thing he does* is run to his brother and tell him about Jesus.

That encounter with Christ affected him so much, it changed him so much, it rocked his world so much that the first thing he does is share this Jesus with his brother. His family.

For most people, there's something incredibly intimidating about talking about your relationship with Jesus with your family.

Or even more awkward: asking them about their relationship with Jesus.

That shouldn't be the case, that was not God's design.

In fact, the Church explains that the family was created to be "the domestic church", and parents designated as the "first preachers of the faith to their children"[30].

But more and more people admit that the hardest place to talk about their faith is in their home, with their family. If that's true for you, take comfort in knowing that you are not alone in that struggle and pray for the courage to share your faith with your family. Attempt to overcome the awkwardness of the situation by regularly initiating conversations about religion, spirituality and faith.

If you grew up in a home where faith, prayer, and religion were a shared experience, consider yourself incredibly blessed. Be sure to thank your parents for instilling that biblical, righteous value in your family.

Regardless of your situation, if your relationship with Jesus is the most important thing in your life, don't you want to talk about it with the people you love the most?

If He's transformed who you are, wouldn't you want to share that life-changing truth with those closest to you?

---

[30] Pope Paul VI, Lumen Gentium, 11

YOUR FRIENDS.

Jesus wasn't done calling people to follow Him. The action continues the next day as Jesus leaves Galilee:

> **"Finding Philip, he said to him, 'Follow me.' [and] Philip found Nathanael and told him, 'We have found the one Moses wrote about in the Law, and about whom the prophets also wrote.' "**
>
> *John 1:43-46*

Jesus finds Philip, and after Philip realizes who Jesus is, the very first thing he does is find his best friend Nathanael and tell him about Jesus[31].

He knows Jesus, and he wants his closest friend to know Him too. Not out of obligation, but out of love for him.

Philip realized just how game-changing this encounter with Jesus was. He realized that his life would never be the same. He realized from this point on, everything was BETTER than it had been.

Once Philip made this realization, he didn't hesitate to tell Nathanael about it because he wanted his friend to be blessed, transformed and renewed in the same way!

Don't you want the same for your best friends?

You're not sharing your faith with your friends out of a spirit of judgment: you're not condemning them. You're sharing your faith with them because you have found

---

[31] Notice that it's Jesus who finds Philip. It's never the other way around. We never "find Jesus" because He is never lost. We are always found by Him.

something so incredible that you want them to experience it as well!

Is it hard to talk about your faith with your friends?

Are they open/receptive to the topic?

Do they know about your relationship with Christ?

Do you know about theirs?

EVERYONE YOU KNOW.

It's the middle of a hot day in Samaria, and a woman is heading to the well in the center of town to draw water. We don't know a lot about her, except that she is an outcast. No one draws water in the middle of the day, it's far too hot for that. No one except people who are trying to avoid their neighbors.

When this outcast arrives at the well, she finds Jesus waiting there for her.

> **"Jesus said to her, 'Give me a drink.' The Samaritan woman said to him, 'How can you, a Jew, ask me, a Samaritan woman, for a drink?' "**
>
> *John 4:7,9*

As their conversation continues, Jesus reveals his identity to her. He explains that He is the Messiah, the source of "living water".

When the Samaritan woman realizes who Jesus is, *the very first thing she does* is rush off to tell everyone she knows. She doesn't just tell her friends (she might not even have any), she tells the whole town.

"Many of the Samaritans of that town began to believe in him because of the word of the woman who testified..."

John 4:39

Her experience with Jesus was so powerful, that she told <u>EVERYONE SHE KNEW</u>.

She didn't filter it. She didn't make a judgement call that certain people didn't need to hear about Him or wouldn't want to listen to her story, she told <u>EVERYONE</u>.

<u>EVERYONE</u> is a hard concept for most us to grasp. Most of the time, when it comes to talking about our faith, we automatically put people into categories.

OPEN	People who love us and would love to hear about Jesus!
CLOSED	People who could care less about this Jesus-thing. They'd be annoyed, maybe even angry if we tried to talk to them about it.
HATERS	People who just flat out hate us and don't want to talk to us about anything (especially Jesus).
CHURCH PEOPLE	People who already know and love Jesus, so talking to them would be a waste of time.
EXPERTS	People who know more than us about Jesus, Catholicism, Scripture, etc. It would be embarrassing to talk to them because they'd make us feel stupid.

The funny thing is when we categorize people like this, we have a hard time putting anyone in the OPEN category, but it's really easy to fill the other categories.

What's even funnier is that categories don't matter.

The Samaritan women didn't go share her encounter with OPEN people (there probably weren't any). She shared her story with EVERYONE.

We're called to do the same: Forget about categories. Forget about labels. Just tell people about Jesus.

> **"Jesus teaches us that the Good News, which he brings, is not reserved to one part of humanity, it is to be communicated to everyone."**
>
> *Pope Francis* [32]

EVERYONE. EVERY WHERE.

When Jesus commanded us to "make disciples of all nations"[33], He intended for us to go beyond our circle.

He expected us to step out of our comfort zone and share the Gospel with everyone we meet.

Even more, He commands us to INTENTIONALLY step out of our comfort zones AND go out into the world to share the Gospel.

---

[32] Pope Francis, Angelus on January 26, 2014

[33] Matthew 28:19

"Christ commands us to be his witnesses to the ends of the earth...to proclaim his Good News to all people, everywhere and at all times."

USCCB [34]

Have you ever considered going as a missionary to a foreign country?

Ever thought about serving in an inner city parish where you can share your faith with people you would have never met otherwise?

Ever spent some time on the street with the marginalized?

Maybe you should.

Maybe that's where Jesus is calling you.

---

[34] United States Conference of Catholic Bishops, Committee on Evangelization and Catechesis, "Disciples Called to Witness: The New Evangelization"

THE HOW?

STEP ONE: BRING THEM TO JESUS.

Andrew, Philip, and the Samaritan woman all went about their evangelization the same way: they brought people to Jesus.

Andrew grabbed his brother Simon and **"brought him to Jesus"**[35].

Philip found Nathanael and told him to **"come and see"** this Jesus he had met[36].

Likewise, after her conversation with Jesus, the Samaritan woman ran into town and told everyone to **"come see"** this man who knew everything about her[37].

They did not engage in a deep theological argument.

They did not recite Scripture.

They simply shared their story, their encounter with one simple goal in mind: bring their listeners to meet Jesus.

They weren't trying to convince anyone of anything, they just wanted other people to have the same encounter with the Lord that they had.

They each realized something very important: there's nothing we can ever say to change a person's heart.

Life change, heart change, comes only from Jesus.

It's simply our job to get people to Him.

---

[35] John 1:42

[36] John 1:46

[37] John 4:29

STEP TWO: LET JESUS DO THE REST.

Once Andrew brings Simon to Jesus, Andrew doesn't say a word: he let's Jesus do the rest.

When Philip gets Nathanael before Jesus, he says nothing: he let's Jesus do the rest.

After the Samaritan woman has told her story and brought the entire town to Jesus, she let Jesus do the rest.

And **"many more began to believe in Him"** – not because of her testimony, but **"because of His word"**[38].

> **"We no longer believe because of your word; for we have heard for ourselves, and we know that this is truly the savior of the world."**
>
> *John 4:42*

EASIER SAID THEN DONE.

Your role is simple, just one step: bring them to Jesus. Except that's way easier said then done, right?

What exactly does that mean? How do I do that in the real world? What does that look like for me: In my school? At the office? With my friends? In my family? Among my enemies?

Let's figure that out. After all, this book would be pretty worthless if it told you that you were supposed to be an evangelist but didn't have any practical advice or tips for doing so, right?

---

[38] John 4:41

TIP #1: KNOW YOUR STORY.

People far from God don't care what the Bible says. They don't care what the Church teaches. All of that is irrelevant to them. If someone is having a conversation with you, then what they care about is you.

> **"Evangelization does not consist in proselytizing, but in attracting by our witness those who are far off…"**
>
> *Pope Francis* [39]

If people look at you and realize there's something different about you, if there's something they see in you that they want for themselves (joy, hope, love, peace, etc.[40]), they'll want to know your story.

If they see that your faith is important to you – they'll want to know "Why?".

When they find out you go to church every Sunday – they'll want to know "Why?".

If you tell them you love Jesus – they'll want to know "Why?".

They don't want you to open up a Bible and quote Scripture to them, they want to know <u>YOUR</u> story. In <u>YOUR</u> words. From <u>YOUR</u> heart.

It doesn't matter to them what Scripture says. It doesn't matter to them what the Church teaches. It doesn't matter to them what you've read.

---

[39] Pope Francis, Mass for the Evangelization of Peoples on July 7, 2015

[40] You know, the "Fruits of the Spirit" which (if you're a follower of Christ) should be evident in your life.

What matters to them is how this Jesus has transformed YOUR life.

What matters to them is YOUR STORY. So be ready to share that story with them.

Work through it ahead of time: Know your story.

More than that, know how to tell it in a way that is clear, truthful, and free from church lingo or jargon.

> **"Always be prepared to give an answer to everyone who asks you to give the reason for the hope that you have."**
> *1 Peter 3:15*

TIP #2:
LOVE THEM FIRST.

It's all well and good if you have your story. If you've worked it out perfectly. If you know it backwards and forwards. You should. Well done. But that story is useless if no one wants to hear it.

I've recently learned something in my life, an important principle that should have been obvious, but apparently I never caught: if you're a jerk, **no one cares what you have to say**.

See, people want to be loved. They want to spend time with people who love them. They want to listen to the words and the stories of people who love them.

But here's the catch: you don't love people so that you can bring them to Jesus, because when you do that, you have an ulterior motive. Your love isn't genuine.

You love people because they deserve it.

You love people because they were created in the image and likeness of God.

You love people because Christ commands you to[41].

You love people because Jesus loves people.

Our constant prayer should be that our hearts break for those whom the heart of God breaks. You know what? Every single person, every man, woman and child (especially those who are far from God): Jesus' heart breaks for them.

He loves them.

If we are going to be followers of Christ, we need to love the people of God <u>before anything else</u>.

In doing so, we will bear fruit.

It is through that love, that relationship that opportunity presents itself.

When our focus is on loving people first, we will no doubt have the opportunity to share our stories with them and bring them to Jesus.

TIP #3:
SPEAK THE NAME OF JESUS.

It's far too easy for us to tell our story and take the credit. It's even easier to tell our story and give credit to a generic "god":

"God has blessed my life."

---

[41] John 13:34-35

"God has changed my world."

"God has made such a difference."

All of which are true, but the thing is we're not just trying to bring people before "God"; we're not just trying to bring people to encounter a spiritual being.

We're trying to introduce them to **JESUS**.

It's **JESUS** who died on a cross for us.

It's **JESUS** whose love changes our lives.

It's **JESUS** who transforms hearts.

It's **JESUS** who brings healing.

It's **JESUS** who offers forgiveness.

It's **JESUS** who bids us "come and follow me".

It's **JESUS**.

For a lot of us, myself included, there's almost something awkward about using the name of Jesus.

Something just a little weird about slipping His name into conversation.

We find ourselves generalizing Him–calling Him "God", so we don't offend anyone or make people uncomfortable.

But if we want to be people who are bringing others to Jesus, *we have to use His name*!

Can you introduce your best friend to someone without using her name?

Can you introduce someone to Jesus without using His name?

No. If we're going to bring someone to Jesus, we have to call Him by name–and there is so much power in that name[42]!

In your life, are you using the name of Jesus?

Are you speaking the name of Jesus or are you speaking in generalities?

When people want to know your story, they want to know how JESUS changed your life. They don't want to know how "god" came into your life and changed things because they can find "gods" in a lot of different places.

They want to know about **JESUS**.

How **JESUS** changed your life.

How **JESUS** has become the focus of your life.

If you don't speak **HIS NAME**, they will never hear it. And if they don't know His name, if no one has spoken it to them, then they will never know Him.

People cannot know Jesus without first knowing His name.

---

[42] Philippians 2:9-10

TIP #4:
USE WORDS.

Every time I say this I make enemies, but it needs to be said.

One of the biggest blows to evangelization by Catholics is the misattributed quote: **"Preach the gospel at all times; when necessary, use words"**[43].

It's a cute quote. And it does make an important point: you have to live out the Gospel by your actions. But it also contradicts Scripture. Nowhere in Scripture does Jesus say, "Go into the whole world and be nice to everyone", but rather:

> **"Go into the whole world and proclaim the gospel to every creature."**
>
> *Matthew 16:15*

Proclaim the Gospel. Not "mirror" the Gospel. Or "live out" the Gospel. **Proclaim** the Gospel.

Yes, we're supposed to do good works[44]. Yes, we're supposed to clothe the naked, feed the hungry, visit the sick[45].

---

[43] **St. Francis did not say that.** There's no record of him ever saying anything like that. Judging from the what we know he said and did, it would be hard to believe that those words would have come from St. Francis. He did not model that "use words when necessary" philosophy in his own life: he was a **preacher**. No, St. Francis was ***an incredible preacher***, often preaching in as many as five villages in a single day. St. Francis instructed his followers to do likewise: preach a Gospel of sin and repentance everywhere they went. **For St. Francis, words were definitely a necessity in preaching the Gospel.**

[44] James 2:17

[45] Matthew 25:34-40

Yes, we're supposed to care for widows and orphans[46].

All of those are evidence of our faith, but they don't replace the great commission: **Proclaim** the Gospel.

How are people going to come to believe in the Gospel-in Jesus Christ-if we don't use words to tell the world of His glory? To tell the world our story of how He changed our lives?

> **"How, then, can they call on the one they have not believed in? And how can they believe in the one of whom they have not heard? And how can they hear without someone preaching to them? And how can anyone preach unless they are sent?"**
>
> *Romans 10:14*

When we read that verse, we agree with the logic. We see how each verse connects to the next. It makes sense. But when we get to the last verse, we think we've found a loophole. That's not me: I wasn't called to preach, I wasn't sent out to do that. Paul must be talking about someone else.

Sorry, you don't get off that easy. Remember: He created each one of us to go out and "make disciples of all nations"[47].

That includes you.

Preach the Gospel at all times; and <u>always</u> use words.

---

[46] James 1:27

[47] Matthew 28:19

THE RESULT?

WHAT IF YOU KEPT SILENT?

A video that made it's way around YouTube a few years back featured a well-know magician, Penn Jillette. Penn is an outspoken and firm atheist. The video is his response to a man who shared his faith in Christ with Penn after a show.

Before we get to Penn's response, I wanted to talk about how this man evangelized (or as Penn calls it, **proselytized**[48]) Penn:

The man approaches Penn after a show and strikes up a conversation with him about how much he enjoyed the show. Then at the end of the conversation, he hands Penn a bible with a message to Penn inscribed inside. In the video, Penn notes how genuine and sincere the man was: that he felt as if the man truly cared about him.

He didn't attack Penn for his beliefs. He didn't condemn him. He loved him and shared his love for Christ with him.

Back to Penn's response. It would be cool to say that because of this man's witness, Penn is now a believer, a follower of Christ: he's not.

But maybe his unwavering atheism makes his response even more powerful.

> **"I've always said that I don't respect people who don't proselytize. I don't respect that at all. If you believe that there's a heaven and a hell, and people**

---

[48] Defined by Mr. Webster as "To convert or attempt to convert (someone) from one religion, belief, or opinion to another."

could be going to hell or not getting eternal life, and you think that it's not really worth telling them this because it would make it socially awkward...

How much do you have to hate somebody to not proselytize? How much do you have to hate somebody to believe that everlasting life is possible and not tell them that?

I mean, if I believed, beyond the shadow of a doubt, that a truck was coming at you, and you didn't believe that truck was bearing down on you, there is a certain point where I tackle you. And this is more important than that."

Penn Jillette [49]

Do you believe in the IMPORTANCE of the Gospel?

Do you believe in the POWER of the Gospel?

Do you believe in the LIFE promised by the Gospel?

Philip believed. Andrew believed. Peter believed.

Do you?

If you do, how can you keep silent?

---

[49] You can find the video on YouTube by searching for **"Penn Jillette proselytize"**. Note that the video might be offensive to some people.

> **"Whoever hears my word and believes in the one who sent me has eternal life and will not come to condemnation, but has passed from death to life."**
>
> *John 5:24*

If we are not preaching the Word, if we're not sharing the Gospel, think about how many people miss out on eternal life because of our silence.

If we were talking about a speeding truck instead of condemnation, would you speak up? Would you scream out a warning? Would you tackle someone to save them?

Is Penn Jillette right? Is this more important than that?

If so, how can you keep silent?

WHAT IF YOU SHARED THE GOSPEL?

> **"How narrow the gate and constricted the road that leads to life. And those who find it are few."**
>
> *Matthew 7:14*

That narrow gate is Jesus. That "constricted" road is Jesus. Jesus is the path to eternal life. And only a few people find that path, that road, that gate. Only a few people find Jesus.

Not because Jesus is hiding, not even because He's hard to find. Few people find Jesus because there are so few people pointing others to Him.

So what if we all pointed people to Him? What if we all told people about Jesus? What if we all shared our faith, our stories with those around us?

What if that narrow gate, that constricted road were overcrowded? What if those who found it were MANY (not few)?

What if our churches were overflowing? What if we were constantly having to add additional masses and build bigger buildings?

What if more and more people were being transformed by Gospel? What if lives were being restored by encounters with Jesus?

All those things ARE possible. And it doesn't start on an institutional level. We don't have to wait for our parish, our diocese, or the Vatican to institute some sort of "evangelism plan".

It starts with us.

It starts with us loving people, sharing our story with them, and bringing them to Jesus.

The craziest thing is, when we start evangelizing, the growth we'll see isn't simple addition: we're not just adding one person and then another person.

Evangelism is **EXPONENTIAL**. When we bring someone to Jesus, and He transforms their life, they won't be able to contain it. Like Peter, they'll have to share it!

> **"It is impossible for us not to speak about what we have seen and heard."**
> *Acts 4:20*

"Go and announce the Gospel of the Lord."

Concluding Rites of the Mass [50]

---

[50] The Roman Missal, Third Edition. "Concluding Rites". "Dismissal".

Michael Marchand is a Catholic missionary, evangelist, author, and co-founder of ProjectYM – an organization dedicated to equipping Catholic youth ministers. Through ProjectYM, Michael travels around the world preaching the Gospel and training ministry leaders.

Michael has a theology degree from Loyola University Chicago and currently lives in Houston, TX with his wife, Crystal, and their children – Noah, Ruth, and Esther.

FOLLOW MICHAEL

MichaelMarchand
TWITTER

MichaelWMarchand
INSTAGRAM

For more information about bringing Michael and his team to speak at your parish or event, head to:
http://projectym.com/booking

projectYM
PROJECTYM.COM